one bowl
allergy free baking

Linda Bosnic is a mother of two young boys, passionate cook and advocate for organic, fresh and additive-free food. She created the simple and delicious recipes in this book after a nephew was diagnosed with severe food allergies.

Linda lives in Melbourne. She has published articles in *Melbourne's Child* magazine and *Reader's Digest*.

For Luke and Nicholas, may you always enjoy happiness, good health, great food – and know that I love you.

one bowl
allergy free baking

Linda Bosnic

Wakefield
Press

Wakefield Press
1 The Parade West
Kent Town
South Australia 5067
www.wakefieldpress.com.au

First published 2010
Reprinted 2011

Edited by Julia Beaven, Wakefield Press
Designed by Mark Thomas
Typeset by Clinton Ellicott, Wakefield Press
Printed in Australia by Griffin Press, Adelaide

National Library of Australia Cataloguing-in-Publication entry
Author: Bosnic, Linda Joy.
Title: One bowl allergy free baking/Linda Joy Bosnic.
ISBN: 978 1 86254 909 8 (pbk.).
Subjects: Baking.
                   Food allergy – Diet therapy – Recipes.
Dewey Number: 641.815

Government
of South Australia

Arts SA

foreword

As parents, we experience both immense joy and immense responsibilities, and so we look for things that can help us with the challenges of raising our children.

Allergies have been a part of my family for decades. I have three children and we recently found that my son Antonio was diagnosed with anaphalaxis to nuts. In a traumatic experience, we saw the sudden danger posed to his health by simply eating a peanut butter sandwich. And so life has changed for us and little Antonio, we must now be vigilant in making sure he avoids foods that can trigger a dangerous reaction.

Linda's allergy free baking book will be a welcome tool for parents such as myself and I hope it provides some comfort for other parents who are looking for simple and safe recipes for their children.

Wiggle on and bake on everybody!

Anthony Field from The Wiggles

contents

Acknowledgements

There are many people to thank for their help in this project. My mum, Joy, and sister, Jen, for their encouragement and support, for believing in my book and their many hours of test baking to ensure these recipes were a success. A big thank you to my husband, Allister, and two boys, Luke and Nicholas, for the lack of complaint when I took over the kitchen to test recipes and sometimes couldn't prepare dinner.

I owe enormous gratitude to Wakefield Press and in particular my fabulous editor, Julia Beaven. Julia immediately connected with my book and has made the publishing process an extremely enjoyable one. Big thanks to Brent Parker-Jones, a gifted and generous photographer; and to my good friend, Margaret, who helped and supported me for many years. To all my supportive friends who were there to help with babysitting duties, thank you very much.

Finally, I would like to thank my father, Maurie Ryding, who passed away over six years ago. He instilled in me that it was important to follow your dreams and if you worked hard, anything was possible. I love you, Dad.

introduction

Nearly 10 years ago, my nephew Lachlan was diagnosed with anaphylaxis to nuts, dairy and egg. My sister and her family knew little about food allergies and entered a strange and sometimes lonely world. For many years at friends' birthday parties Lachlan could eat only his special food brought from home, never able to join with other children to eat birthday cake. The view by most people was that any allergy-free baked goods were either too difficult to make or were inedible.

A few years later it was time for celebrations when my first child arrived. I was determined Lachlan would enjoy a normal party experience so I ensured that all the food (even for the adults) was nut, dairy and egg free – especially the birthday cake. I will never forget the look of delight on his face when he was told he could eat anything he wanted from the table and share the birthday cake with everyone else. That was the moment I decided I wanted to do something to help Lachlan, and all those with food allergies.

I have had a passion for baking since I was a child. My mum was a wonderful cook and spent many Saturday afternoons patiently teaching me her skills, but when it came to baking a cake without eggs or biscuits without butter I must admit I was a little daunted. I searched for cookbooks but the only recipes I could find were complicated, had unusual ingredients and took too long to make. I tried many of these recipes but, frustrated by the poor results, decided that there must be a better way.

So I started to develop my own recipes and as I was now a busy mother of two young boys, all the recipes had to be extremely quick and easy. I didn't have time to fuss around with an electric mixer so I made sure the recipes didn't need one. I kept the list of ingredients short so I didn't need to waste time walking the aisles of supermarkets. And I utilised the most honest taste testers around – my boys.

Over the years I have shared my cakes, biscuits and slices with many others and I watch the looks of surprise when I tell them the food is so quick to make and allergy free. And I realised I was making these recipes all the time as they were so easy and delicious, even though my family was not affected by food allergies.

All of the recipes in this book are nut-free, dairy-free and egg-free and there are also many recipes suited to those with a wheat allergy or gluten intolerance. I hope *One bowl allergy-free baking* will encourage people (whether affected by allergies or not) back into the kitchen so no one need miss the delights of freshly baked treats warm from the oven.

How to ensure these recipes are easy and fast

In order to ensure these recipes remain simple, it helps to follow the steps below.

1. Always start with a tidy kitchen and bench space – very important!
2. Locate your ingredients and have them ready to use.
3. Locate your mixing bowl, baking trays, measuring cups, measuring spoons and have them ready to use.

By following these steps, you can complete the recipes successfully in the times stated in each recipe.

Preparing your work space for allergy-free baking

It only takes a few minutes at the start of cooking to prepare your work space and ensure there are no issues with cross contamination.

1. Wipe down all bench tops and work areas with a clean sponge or cloth.
2. Wash your hands with soap and dry well.
3. Ensure all bowls and utensils to be used have been cleaned well.
4. Avoid using any wooden spoons or boards for allergy-free food preparation unless they are only used for allergy-free cooking. These can contain traces of previously cooked food and be a source of cross contamination.
5. Ensure no allergens accidentally come into contact with the food during preparation. For example, don't make your cup of tea with milk near your cookie dough.

Helpful baking tips

1. Always measure ingredients properly, don't guesstimate!
2. When making a 'wet and dry' recipe, mix the dry ingredients thoroughly, ensuring that no lumps of sugar or other ingredients remain.
3. When incorporating wet ingredients into dry ingredients, use a gentle mixing motion until the ingredients form a batter. Try not to over mix or under mix.
4. For cake recipes, tap the filled cake pan on a flat bench top immediately prior to placing in the oven. This will assist any air bubbles to rise to the surface.
5. Where possible, place your trays on the centre rack of the oven. If using more than one tray, space them evenly and do not overcrowd the oven.
6. Avoid opening the oven door until near the end of the recipe time stated (unless you can see that it needs to be removed earlier).

Gluten-free baking

The recipes in this book that can be made gluten free are highlighted with a gluten-free option icon. The cake-type recipes will have a denser result and are best made on the day of serving. The biscuits, slices and desserts produce similar results to the standard recipe and have similar storage times. It is always important to check the formulations of all ingredients in a recipe as manufacturers can change their products without notice.

Oven temperatures and measures

All recipes have been baked at the temperatures stated in a fan-forced oven so if you are not using a fan-forced oven increase temperatures by 10–20 degrees. As all ovens vary, you may need to adjust temperatures slightly up or down to suit your individual needs.

The following standard Australian measures have been used:

1 cup	=	250 ml
1 tablespoon	=	20 ml
1 teaspoon	=	5 ml

Ingredient descriptions and substitutions

Below are some of the most common ingredients in the recipes and possible substitutions if required. Always check food labels to ensure the ingredient is completely free of nut, dairy and egg as formulations can change without notice. If unsure, call the manufacturer for confirmation.

Chocolate

Two types of dairy-free, nut-free chocolate are currently available in Australia. Kinnerton chocolate is a dark-type chocolate in block form and is imported from the UK. Sweet William chocolate is a milder chocolate available in both blocks and chocolate chips. It is found in most supermarkets and is Australian made and owned. Both will work well in these recipes however always check the ingredient labels before using.

Flour

Unless stated, all flour and self-raising flour used is white. Wholemeal flours are used in some recipes and generally result in a heavier finished product. No sifting of flour is mentioned and all recipes work extremely well without sifting. However if you have the time, sifting can give a slightly lighter finished result.

Gluten-free flour

Many of the recipes work well by substituting the standard wheat flour with gluten-free flour and this has been indicated in the recipes. A variety of pre-blended plain and self-raising gluten-free flours can be found in major supermarkets or health food stores.

Cornflour

Neither cornflour (*milled* maize/corn) nor corn flour (*ground* maize/corn) should contain gluten. However if they have not been exclusively processed (i.e. no other products are made on the production line), they may contain traces of gluten. It is best to search on the internet and find one that advertises itself as gluten free, or carefully check the label.

Oil

The oil used in these recipes is vegetable oil. Other types of mild oils such as sunflower or canola could be substituted without affecting the result. It is best to avoid strong oils such as olive oil.

Soy milk

This has been used in many recipes. If a soy allergy is present, this could be changed to rice milk. As rice milk can be thinner than soy milk, it may be necessary to slightly reduce the quantity needed in each recipe.

Sugar

If the recipe calls for caster sugar or white sugar, these can generally be interchanged without significant effect. When brown sugar is required, it is firmly packed into the required measure. Natural sugar substitutes such as xylitol or stevia are a great healthy alternative and can also be used successfully.

Biscuits

Some of the recipes require biscuit crumbs and there are many plain biscuits available in supermarkets that are free from nuts, dairy, egg and wheat. Always check the ingredient labels before purchasing as formulations can change without notice.

Dried fruits

The standard supermarket range often has preservatives of some kind added to the fruit. Health food shops or farmers' markets have delicious dried fruits available without the addition of preservatives. However always be mindful of cross-contamination of bulk-packaged dried fruits as these are commonly packed in a facility that also packages nuts. If unsure, contact the manufacturer.

Preparing pans and trays

The easiest way to prepare pans and trays for allergy-free baking is to use non-stick baking paper and paper case liners. Biscuit and slice trays can be lined completely with non-stick baking paper. Line the base of cake tins with non-stick baking paper and use a thick coat of Nuttelex (or other dairy-free spread) or cooking spray on the sides of the tin. Loaf tins can generally be covered completely with non-stick paper. Muffins and cupcakes are best made using paper case liners.

By covering all surfaces of trays and pans with non-stick paper or liners, it reduces the risk of possible contamination if the pans have residual food from previous non-allergy recipes. It also saves time when washing up!

It is much easier to place mixture onto trays and in tins if the baking paper stays in one place. To assist this, place a small amount of Nuttelex or cooking spray directly on the tin and stick the paper to the tin.

Most cupcake and muffin recipes can be made in either the standard 12-hole tray or the smaller 24-hole size. Large and small paper cases are available in the supermarket. Always reduce the cooking time by five to 10 minutes if making the smaller muffin size and be aware that it takes more time to fill 24 smaller holes.

In all cases, the cake recipes can be made in either a standard cake pan or a ring pan. If using the ring pan, cooking time is generally reduced so set oven timer to at least 10 minutes less than the recipe states before testing.

Food storage

Ensure storage containers are clean and have not been used for other food that may contain allergens. If unsure, wash the container and line with non-stick baking paper before storing product.

Cakes, muffins and loaves

These are best stored in an airtight container and generally last about three days (unless stated otherwise in recipe). Cakes and loaves can be tightly wrapped in cling wrap and frozen whole or cut into thick slices and wrapped tightly for freezing. Muffins can also be wrapped tightly and frozen. Defrost individual cake slices or muffins at room temperature for 30 minutes. Whole cakes or loaves should be defrosted overnight. These can be stored successfully in the freezer for about four weeks.

Biscuits

These are best stored in an airtight container and generally last up to one week. The biscuit dough can be stored in the freezer for up to six weeks. Roll the dough into balls and store the balls in an airtight container between layers of non-stick baking paper. To use, remove dough balls from freezer and place on lined baking trays for about 30 minutes to soften prior to baking.

Slices

These are best sliced and stored in an airtight container in the refrigerator. Some slices can be frozen successfully and these are indicated in the recipes.

Food allergies, intolerances and anaphylaxis

It seems that everyone either has or knows someone with a food allergy or intolerance and an increasing number of people are at risk of an anaphylactic reaction, the most severe and life-threatening form of food allergy.

Food allergies occur when the immune system responds to a harmless food as if it were toxic. Symptoms are generally quick to appear, developing within 20 minutes of consuming the food. Most are mild – swelling around the mouth, stomach upsets and skin rashes – however severe anaphylactic reactions can be life-threatening and require immediate treatment. Watch out for breathing difficulties, swelling of the tongue or throat, a persistent cough, difficulty talking, pale skin colour and floppiness or a loss of consciousness. A person suffering a severe reaction requires an immediate injection of adrenaline, which is generally carried by the person in the form of an adrenaline auto-injector. They also require immediate treatment by a medical professional.

Some of the most common food allergy triggers are milk, eggs, peanut, tree nuts, sesame, fish, crustaceans, wheat and soy. These foods trigger 90 per cent of food allergic reactions in Australia. It is estimated that approximately one in 20 children and one in 100 adults have food allergies.

Food intolerances occur when the body has a chemical reaction after eating or drinking a particular food. It is not an immune system response. Symptoms can be immediate, as with allergies, but many take between 12 and 24 hours to develop. The intensity of the reaction can often be related to the amount of food consumed. In many cases, no symptoms appear until a certain amount of the food is eaten. This threshold amount varies from person to person. Reactions can include sweating, hives, headache/migraine, diarrhoea, breathing problems or palpitations. Intolerances have been linked with conditions including asthma, chronic fatigue syndrome and irritable bowel syndrome.

Some of the most common foods that can cause intolerance are dairy products, eggs, flavour enhancers such as MSG, food additives, strawberries, citrus fruits, tomatoes, wine and chocolate.

Food allergies and food intolerances are on the increase worldwide. The best way to treat an allergy or intolerance is to eliminate the food from the diet. Avoidance of the food is the only way to prevent a reaction. Accidental exposure can occur so in the case of anaphylaxis, the person and their caregivers need to be educated in the symptoms and be prepared to give adrenaline if required. Anyone who suspects that they may have a food allergy or intolerance should see their doctor for a correct medical diagnosis.

For further information, go to the Anaphylaxis Australia website which has very comprehensive information on food allergies (www.allergyfacts.org.au).

Allergy-free parties

If you are catering for a child with food allergies, it can be helpful to consider the following:

1. Always call the parents and ask whether it is okay for you to provide food that is suitable for their child. Discuss with them the recipes from this book that you plan to use.
2. Children with food allergies can get nervous about food they are not familiar with so never try to force a food on a child, even if you know it is allergy-free.
3. Try to avoid having food at the party that could possibly cause a severe reaction. Some examples are peanut butter, eggs or cheese-based snacks. It is easy to cater for all children at a party by remembering measures as simple as choosing plain potato crisps instead of cheese-flavoured snacks and baking recipes from this book for all.
4. Be aware of the concern that parents of children with food allergies have in regard to food and parties. Make the parents feel comfortable if they need to stay for the duration of the party.

Artificial ingredients (and how to avoid them)

There are many ingredients commonly used in manufactured food that can have adverse health effects. Food additives in Australia are governed by the Food Standards Code and regulated by Food Standards Australia New Zealand (FSANZ). Many ingredients are approved for use in Australia and considered 'safe' even though their use in other countries may be limited or banned.

Artificial food additives can cause a wide range of health-related issues. Headaches, skin rashes, asthma and behavioural disorders are just a few of the possible effects. Children are generally more susceptible to these problems because they weigh less. Some children can have an immediate reaction to bright food colourings while others may take several days for the effect to surface.

Ideally, we should all try to limit our consumption of food additives however this can be particularly difficult when food choices are already limited by allergies. By using the recipes in this book and baking at home, many of these additives can be avoided as they are commonly found in commercially prepared baked goods. Some of the recipes in this book require ingredients that are extremely difficult to locate without artificial additives of some kind. One example of this would be glace cherries. If additives are of particular concern, it would be best to avoid those particular recipes.

Below is a list of some common artificial ingredients that may need to be avoided and the foods they may be found in.*

Artificial Colours
102, 104, 107, 110, 122, 123, 124, 127, 129, 132, 133, 142, 143, 151, 153, 155, 160b (Annatto), 173, 174, 175

Sorbates
Cheese and cheese-based products, dips, drinks.
200, 201, 202, 203

Benzoates
Soft drinks, cordials, medicine.
210, 211, 212, 213, 216, 218

Sulphites
Dried fruits, cordials, juices, processed meats.
220, 221, 222, 223, 224, 225, 226, 227,228

Nitrates
Cured and processed meats.
They are prohibited for use in food for infants less than 12 months of age.
249, 250, 251, 252

Proprionates
Bread and bakery products.
280, 281, 282, 283

*From Smart Snacks website 2010 www.smartsnacks.com.au.

Artificial Flavours

All should be avoided.

Flavour Enhancers

Flavoured chips, corn chips, popcorn, flavoured savoury biscuits, instant noodle sachets.

620–625	glutames including MSG
627	disodium guanylate
631	disodium inosinate
635	ribonucleotides

Hydrolysed vegetable protein (HVP)

Artificial Sweeteners

951	aspartame

Antioxidants

Oils and fats, baked goods, muesli and snack bars, biscuits.
310, 311, 312, 319, 320, 321, 385

Thickeners

Vegetable gums found in cakes, slices, muffins, smoothies.
407, 466

Anti-caking agents/emulsifiers

431, 433, 435, 436, 530, 553, 900, 914

Miscellaneous

943a, 950, 952, 954, 1201, 1520, 1521

Natural colours and sprinkles can be found in health food stores or online at Smart Snacks (www.smartsnacks.com.au).

one bowl
and
15 minutes

In this section . . .

coconut cake

This easy delicious cake freezes well for snacks! The result is slightly flatter when gluten-free but still tasty.

Preparation time: 10 minutes

....

1 cup desiccated coconut
1 cup SR flour (or gluten-free SR flour)
1 cup caster sugar
1 cup soy milk

....

Preheat oven to 180°C and grease and line a 23 cm x 13 cm loaf tin with non-stick baking paper.

1. Mix dry ingredients in a large bowl.
2. Make a well in centre of dry ingredients and pour in soy milk.
3. Mix together until they form a batter (not too much mixing).
4. Pour into loaf tin and bake for 25–30 minutes or until a skewer inserted into cake comes out clean.
5. Cool in tin for 10 minutes before turning out onto wire rack.
6. Sprinkle with sifted icing sugar or ice with lemon or orange icing (see p. 116).

chocolate banana cake

A delicious way to use up old bananas!

Preparation time: 15 minutes

....

dry   1 cup SR flour
      1/4 cup cocoa
      2/3 cup caster sugar

wet   1/2 cup vegetable oil
      1/2 cup soy milk
      1/2 cup ripe banana, mashed (about 2 small bananas)

....

Preheat oven to 180°C and grease and line a 20 cm cake tin with non-stick baking paper.

1. Mix all dry ingredients in a large bowl.
2. Make a well in centre of dry ingredients and add wet ingredients.
3. Mix together until they form a batter (not too much mixing).
4. Pour into prepared cake tin and bake for 40–45 minutes or until a skewer inserted into cake comes out clean.
5. Cool in cake tin for 10 minutes before turning out onto wire rack.
6. Cake can be iced with chocolate-cream icing (see p. 119).

chocolate cupcakes

This simple but decadent 'wet and dry' recipe is always a hit. The gluten-free version makes denser muffin-like cakes, best baked on the day of serving.

Preparation time: 15 minutes
Servings: About 10–12 cupcakes

....

dry
1¼ cups SR flour (or gluten-free SR flour)
½ cup caster sugar
¼ cup cocoa
½ cup dairy-free, nut-free chocolate chips

wet
⅓ cup vegetable oil
⅔ cup water
1 teaspoon vanilla essence

....

Preheat oven to 170°C and grease and line a 12-hole cupcake/muffin tray with paper cases.

1. Mix dry ingredients in a large bowl.
2. Make a well in centre of dry ingredients and add wet ingredients.
3. Mix together until they form a batter (not too much mixing).
4. Spoon into prepared pan, filling close to the top of each case.
5. Bake for 15–20 minutes or until a skewer inserted into cupcake comes out clean.
6. Cool in tray for 5 minutes before turning out onto wire rack.
7. Once cold, ice with chocolate icing (see p. 117) and decorate as desired.

vanilla cupcakes

These are always a hit at children's parties!

Preparation time: 15 minutes
Servings: About 12 cupcakes

....

dry 2 cups SR flour
¾ cup caster sugar
½ cup brown sugar

wet ⅓ cup vegetable oil
½ cup water
½ cup soy milk
2 teaspoons vanilla essence

....

Preheat oven to 180°C and grease 12-hole cupcake/muffin tray or line with paper cases.

1. Mix dry ingredients in a large bowl.
2. Make a well in centre of dry ingredients and add wet ingredients.
3. Mix together until they form a batter (not too much mixing).
4. Spoon into prepared pan, filling close to the top of each case.
5. Bake for 15–20 minutes or until a skewer inserted into cupcake comes out clean.
6. Cool in tray for 5 minutes before turning out onto wire rack.
7. Once cold, ice with butter-cream icing (see p. 118) and decorate as desired.

double chocolate cake

This cake will satisfy the biggest chocolate craving!

Preparation time: 15 minutes

....

 2 cups SR flour
¾ cup caster sugar
¼ cup cocoa
1 cup dairy-free, nut-free chocolate chips
1 teaspoon baking powder

 1 teaspoon vanilla essence
½ cup vegetable oil
1 cup soy milk

....

Preheat oven to 180°C and grease and line a 20 cm cake tin with non-stick baking paper.

1. Mix dry ingredients in a large bowl.
2. Make a well in centre of dry ingredients and add wet ingredients.
3. Mix together until they form a batter (not too much mixing).
4. Pour into prepared cake tin and bake for 35–40 minutes or until a skewer inserted into cake comes out clean.
5. Cool in cake tin for 10 minutes before turning out onto wire rack.
6. Delicious when iced with chocolate-cream icing (see p. 119).

vanilla sponge cake

A light cake that can be sandwiched together to make a delicious celebration cake.

Preparation time: 15 minutes

....

dry   2 cups SR flour
3 teaspoons baking powder
¾ cup sugar

wet   ¾ cup vegetable oil
1½ cups cold water
2 teaspoons vanilla essence
Jam

....

Preheat oven to 180°C and grease and line two 20 cm cake tins with non-stick baking paper.

1. Mix dry ingredients in a large bowl.
2. Make a well in centre of dry ingredients and add wet ingredients.
3. Mix together until they form a batter (not too much mixing).
4. Pour half of mix into each prepared cake tin and bake for 20–25 minutes or until a skewer inserted into cakes comes out clean.
5. Cool in cake tin for 10 minutes before turning out onto wire rack.
6. Once cool, spread a layer of jam on top of one cake half. Cover jam with butter-cream icing (see p. 118) and put second layer on top. Ice top with sugar or butter-cream icing.

apricot and banana cake

The shredded coconut adds delicious flavour to this cake.

Preparation time: 15 minutes

....

dry 1 cup SR flour
1/4 cup sugar
1 cup dried apricots, diced
1 cup shredded coconut

wet 1 cup ripe banana, mashed (about 3 medium bananas)
1 cup soy milk

....

Preheat oven to 180°C and grease and line a 20 cm cake tin with non-stick baking paper.

1. Mix dry ingredients in a large bowl.
2. Make a well in centre of dry ingredients and add wet ingredients.
3. Mix together until they form a batter (not too much mixing).
4. Pour into prepared cake tin and bake for 50–60 minutes or until a skewer inserted into cake comes out clean.
5. Cool in cake tin for 10 minutes before turning out onto wire rack.
6. Delicious served with honey icing (see p. 121).

afternoon tea cake

This cake is delicious served warm with dairy-free spread on the day it's baked. To freshen up on subsequent days, wrap a slice in paper towel (to stop it going soggy) and microwave for 10–15 seconds.

Preparation time: 15 minutes

1 ½ cups SR flour
½ cup caster sugar
1 cup sultanas
2 tablespoons mixed spice
1 cup black brewed tea, cooled

Preheat oven to 180ºC and grease and line a 23 cm x 13 cm loaf tin with non-stick baking paper.

1. Mix dry ingredients in a large bowl.
2. Make a well in centre of dry ingredients and pour in cooled tea.
3. Mix together until they form a batter (not too much mixing).
4. Pour into loaf tin and bake for 40–45 minutes or until a skewer inserted into loaf comes out clean.
5. Cool in loaf tin for 10 minutes before turning out onto wire rack.

banana cake

Easy, moist and delicious!

Preparation time: 15 minutes

....

dry 2 cups SR flour
¾ cup brown sugar
1 teaspoon mixed spice

wet 1½ cups banana, mashed (about 4 medium bananas)
½ cup vegetable oil
½ cup soy milk

....

Preheat oven to 180°C and grease and line a 20 cm cake tin with non-stick baking paper.

1. Mix dry ingredients in a large bowl.
2. Make a well in centre of dry ingredients and add wet ingredients.
3. Mix together until they form a batter (not too much mixing).
4. Pour into prepared cake tin and bake for 25–30 minutes or until a skewer inserted into cake comes out clean.
5. Cool in tin for 10 minutes before turning out onto wire rack.
6. Delicious iced with honey icing (see p. 121).

spicy carrot cake

This is a lovely light version of a standard carrot cake.

Preparation time: 15 minutes

....

 2 cups SR flour

1 teaspoon baking powder

1 teaspoon cinnamon

½ teaspoon nutmeg

½ cup caster sugar

1 medium carrot, grated

 ⅓ cup vegetable oil

1 cup soy milk

....

Preheat oven to 180°C and grease and line a 20 cm cake tin with non-stick baking paper.

1. Mix dry ingredients in a large bowl.
2. Make a well in centre of dry ingredients and add wet ingredients.
3. Mix together until they form a batter (not too much mixing).
4. Pour into prepared cake tin and bake for 45–50 minutes or until a skewer inserted into cake comes out clean.
5. Cool in cake tin for 10 minutes before turning out onto wire rack.
6. Can be iced with butter-cream icing if desired (see p. 118).

apple spice cake

A lovely addition to a morning tea party.

Preparation time: 15 minutes

....

½ cup Nuttelex (or other dairy-free spread)
½ cup caster sugar
1 tin pie apples (about 400 g), mashed roughly
1 cup sultanas
2 cups SR flour
½ teaspoon cinnamon
½ teaspoon mixed spice

....

Preheat oven to 180°C and grease and line a 20 cm cake tin with non-stick baking paper.

1. Mix Nuttelex and sugar together in a large mixing bowl with a large metal spoon until well combined (use back of spoon to push mix together).
2. Add mashed apples and sultanas and mix well.
3. Add flour and spices to apple mixture. Stir in well.
4. Pour into prepared cake tin and bake for 40–45 minutes or until a skewer inserted into cake comes out clean.
5. Cool in cake tin for 10 minutes before turning out onto wire rack.
6. Cake can be iced with lemon or orange icing (see p. 116).

fruit cake

A great cake at Christmas.

Preparation time: 15 minutes

....

6 cups (about 1 kg) mixed dried fruit
2 cups SR flour (or gluten-free SR flour)
2 cups orange juice
1 teaspoon bicarbonate of soda

....

Preheat oven to 170°C and grease and line a 20 cm cake tin with non-stick
baking paper.

1. Place all ingredients in a large bowl and combine well.
2. Spread mix into prepared cake tin and bake for 60–80 minutes or until a skewer
    inserted into cake comes out clean.
3. Cool in tin for 10 minutes before turning out onto wire rack.
    (If top of cake browns too much before cake is cooked, cover top with a sheet of
    aluminium foil for remainder of cooking time.)

pineapple fruit cake

A lovely moist cake.

Preparation time: 15 minutes

....

dry 2½ cups wholemeal SR flour
   1 teaspoon ground ginger
   2 cups mixed dried fruit

wet 1 can (450 g) crushed pineapple in juice
   1 cup soy milk

....

Preheat oven to 170°C and grease and line a 20 cm cake tin with non-stick baking paper.

1. Mix dry ingredients in a large bowl.
2. Make a well in centre of dry ingredients and add wet ingredients.
3. Mix together until they form a batter (not too much mixing).
4. Spread mix into prepared cake tin and bake for 50–60 minutes or until a skewer inserted into cake comes out clean.
5. Cool in cake tin for 10 minutes before turning out onto wire rack.
   (If top of cake browns too much before cake is ready, cover top with a sheet of aluminium foil for remainder of cooking time.)

choc-chip cookies

An all-time favourite! If making these cookies with gluten-free flour, flatten well as they will not spread much.

Preparation time: 15 minutes
Servings: About 30 cookies

½ cup Nuttelex (or other dairy-free spread)
¼ cup caster sugar
¼ cup brown sugar
1 teaspoon vanilla essence
¼ cup soy milk
2 cups SR flour (or gluten-free SR flour)
½ cup dairy-free, nut-free chocolate chips

Preheat oven to 180°C and grease and line biscuit trays with non-stick baking paper.

1. Mix Nuttelex and sugars together in a large bowl with a large metal spoon until well combined (use back of spoon to push mix together).
2. Add vanilla and soy milk and mix well.
3. Add flour and chocolate chips and mix until well combined.
4. Roll teaspoons of mixture into balls and place on baking trays, allowing room for spreading. Flatten slightly with a fork.
5. Bake for 10–12 minutes or until golden brown.
6. Remove from oven and cool slightly on trays before placing on wire racks to cool.

jam butter drops

A simple buttery biscuit treat.

Preparation time: 15 minutes
Servings: About 40 biscuits

....

1 cup Nuttelex (or other dairy-free spread)
½ cup caster sugar
2 cups SR flour
Jam

....

Preheat oven to 180°C and grease or line biscuit trays with non-stick baking paper.

1. Mix Nuttelex and sugar together in a large bowl with a large metal spoon until well combined (use back of spoon to push mix together).
2. Stir in flour and mix with clean hands to form a soft dough.
3. Roll teaspoons of mixture into balls and place on baking trays, allowing room for spreading. Flatten slightly with the back of a spoon.
4. Make an indent with your finger on top of each biscuit and spoon a small amount of jam onto the top of each biscuit.
5. Bake for 12–15 minutes or until biscuits start to brown.
6. Remove from oven and cool slightly on trays before placing on wire racks to cool.

golden caramel bites

A very simple, tasty biscuit. If making these with gluten-free flour, flatten well as they will not spread much.

Preparation time: 15 minutes
Servings: About 25 biscuits

....

½ cup brown sugar
½ cup Nuttelex (or other dairy-free spread)
2 tablespoons golden syrup
1½ cups SR flour (or gluten-free SR flour)

....

Preheat oven to 180°C and grease or line biscuit trays with non-stick baking paper.

1. Mix together sugar and Nuttelex in a large bowl with a large metal spoon until well combined (use back of spoon to push mix together).
2. Add golden syrup and mix well.
3. Stir in flour and mix well to form a soft dough (use back of spoon to push mix together).
4. Roll teaspoons of mix into balls and place on baking trays, allowing room for spreading. Flatten slightly with a fork.
5. Bake for 10–12 minutes or until lightly golden brown.
6. Remove from oven and cool slightly on trays before placing on wire racks to cool.

chocolate cornflake cookies

A crunchy chocolate cookie.

Preparation time: 15 minutes
Servings: About 20 cookies

¾ cup Nuttelex (or other dairy-free spread)
⅔ cup caster sugar
½ teaspoon vanilla essence
1 tablespoon cocoa
1¼ cups plain flour (or gluten-free plain flour)
½ cup cornflakes, crushed (or gluten-free cornflakes)

Preheat oven to 180°C and grease or line biscuit trays with non-stick baking paper.

1. Mix Nuttelex and sugar together in a large mixing bowl with a large metal spoon until well combined (use back of spoon to push mix together).
2. Add all other ingredients and mix together well.
3. Roll teaspoons of mixture into balls and place on baking trays, allowing room between each for spreading. Flatten each ball slightly with a fork.
4. Bake for 12–15 minutes or until edges of biscuits start to brown.
5. Remove from oven and cool slightly on trays before placing on wire racks to cool.

banana biscuits

A soft chewy cookie made with no flour. They are best stored in an airtight container in the refrigerator – if there are any left over.

Preparation time: 15 minutes
Servings: About 24 biscuits

1 cup ripe banana, mashed (about 3 medium bananas)
1 teaspoon vanilla essence
⅓ cup vegetable oil
2 cups rolled oats (or gluten-free rolled oats)
¼ cup sultanas
¼ cup caster sugar
1 teaspoon mixed spice

Preheat oven to 180°C and grease or line biscuit trays with non-stick baking paper.

1. Place all ingredients in a large bowl and combine well.
2. Spoon tablespoons of mix onto baking trays, allowing room for spreading.
3. Press down lightly with a fork.
4. Bake for 12–15 minutes or until golden brown.
5. Remove from oven and cool slightly on trays before placing on wire racks to cool.

chocolate cookies

A rich chocolate treat made with less sugar than you'd think.

Preparation time: 15 minutes
Servings: About 20 cookies

....

½ cup Nuttelex (or other dairy-free spread)
¼ cup sugar
1 cup SR flour
¼ cup cocoa

....

Preheat oven to 180°C and grease or line biscuit trays with non-stick baking paper.

1. Mix Nuttelex and sugar together in a large mixing bowl with a large metal spoon until well combined (use back of spoon to push mix together).
2. Stir in the flour and cocoa and combine well.
3. Roll teaspoons of mixture into balls and place on baking trays, allowing room between each for spreading. Flatten each ball slightly with a fork.
4. Bake for 10–15 minutes or until edges are slightly browned.
5. Remove from oven and cool slightly on trays before removing to cool on wire racks.

chocolate slice

This delicious slice is so easy to make and the ingredients are generally in the cupboard.

Preparation time: 15 minutes
Servings: About 20 squares

....

3 Weet-Bix, crushed
½ cup sugar
½ cup SR flour
½ cup desiccated coconut
1 tablespoon cocoa
½ cup Nuttelex (or other dairy-free spread), melted
Sprinkles

....

Preheat oven to 180°C and grease or line a 20 cm square baking tray with non-stick baking paper.

1. Mix dry ingredients in a large bowl.
2. Add melted Nuttelex and mix well.
3. Press into tin using back of metal spoon and bake for 15–20 minutes or until lightly browned.
4. Ice with chocolate icing (see p. 117) while still warm and decorate with sprinkles.
5. Cool in tray then cut into squares when cold.

chocolate brownies

Moist and decadent – these won't last long.

Preparation time: 15 minutes
Servings: About 20 pieces

⋯⋯⋯⋯⋯⋯⋯⋯⋯⋯⋯⋯⋯⋯⋯⋯⋯⋯⋯⋯⋯⋯⋯⋯⋯⋯

¾ cup (about 100 g) dairy-free, nut-free chocolate
¾ cup Nuttelex (or other dairy-free spread)
1 cup brown sugar
3 tablespoons soy milk
1 teaspoon vanilla essence
1½ cups SR flour

⋯⋯⋯⋯⋯⋯⋯⋯⋯⋯⋯⋯⋯⋯⋯⋯⋯⋯⋯⋯⋯⋯⋯⋯⋯⋯

Preheat oven to 190°C and grease and line a 20 cm square baking tray with non-stick baking paper.

1. Break the chocolate into small pieces and place in medium heatproof bowl with Nuttelex.
2. Microwave on high for 1 minute. Stir well to combine. If not quite melted, heat for further intervals of 30 seconds on high until completely melted.
3. Add the sugar, soy milk and vanilla to melted mixture and stir well.
4. Add flour to wet ingredients and mix.
5. Spread into prepared tray and bake for 20–25 minutes until cooked but still a little moist.
6. Cool in tray then cut into slices.

chocolate fruit munchies

An easy treat to make without turning the oven on!

Preparation time: 15 minutes
Servings: About 20 squares

....

1 cup rice bubbles (or gluten-free rice bubbles)
½ cup desiccated coconut
¼ cup chopped dried fruit (e.g. apricots, peaches, pears)
1½ cups (about 200 g) dairy-free, nut-free chocolate, melted

....

Prepare a 20 cm square baking tray by greasing and lining with non-stick baking paper.

1. Melt chocolate by breaking into small pieces and placing in a large mug or small heatproof bowl in microwave for 1 minute on high. Stir well and if needed, heat again in intervals of 30 seconds on high until completely melted.
2. Mix together the rice bubbles, coconut and dried fruit in a large bowl.
3. Add melted chocolate to other ingredients and mix well.
4. Spread mix into prepared tray in a thin layer using back of metal spoon.
5. Refrigerate until set then cut into squares.
6. Store in an airtight container in the refrigerator.

gingerbread squares

This gingerbread cake has a lovely delicate texture and flavour.

Preparation time: 15 minutes
Servings: About 25 squares

....

½ cup Nuttelex (or other dairy-free spread)
½ cup brown sugar
1 tablespoon golden syrup
3 teaspoons ground ginger
1¼ cups SR flour
½ teaspoon bicarbonate of soda
½ cup warm water

....

Preheat oven to 170°C and grease and line a 20 cm square baking tray with non-stick baking paper.

1. Mix together Nuttelex and sugar in a large bowl with a large metal spoon until well combined (use back of spoon to push mix together).
2. Add golden syrup and ginger and mix well.
3. Stir through flour, bicarbonate of soda and water until they form a light batter (not too much mixing).
4. Spread into prepared tray and bake for 20–25 minutes or until a skewer inserted into cake comes out clean.
5. Cool in tray for 10 minutes before turning out onto wire rack.

oat and honey squares

Preparation time: 15 minutes
Servings: About 20 squares

....

dry   ½ cup wholemeal SR flour
½ cup desiccated coconut
1 cup rolled oats
1 cup sultanas
½ cup sugar

wet   ¾ cup Nuttelex
1 tablespoon honey

....

Preheat oven to 170°C and grease and line a 20 cm square baking tray with non-stick baking paper.

1. Combine all dry ingredients in a large bowl and mix together.
2. Place Nuttelex and honey in a large mug or small heatproof bowl in microwave on high for 30 seconds. Stir until melted and return to microwave for intervals of 10 seconds if necessary.
3. Make a well in centre of dry ingredients and pour in wet ingredients.
4. Mix together until they form a batter.
5. Press evenly into prepared tin (use back of metal spoon to help with spreading).
6. Bake for 15–20 minutes or until golden.
7. Allow to cool in tray for 10 minutes then cut into squares while still warm. Cool completely before removing from tray.

quick fruit slice

Easy, light and fruity! The gluten-free version makes quite a moist mix but works well if you add an extra 10 minutes to the cooking time.

Preparation time: 10 minutes
Servings: About 20 slices

1 cup SR flour (or gluten-free SR flour)
1 cup brown sugar
½ cup rolled oats (or gluten-free rolled oats)
1 cup sultanas
½ cup desiccated coconut
1 cup soy milk

Preheat oven to 180°C and grease and line a 28 cm x 18 cm baking tray with non-stick baking paper.

1. Mix dry ingredients in a large bowl.
2. Make a well in centre of dry ingredients and pour in soy milk.
3. Mix together until they form a batter (not too much mixing).
4. Spread into prepared tray and bake for 20–25 minutes or until golden brown (careful not to overcook).
5. Cool in tray completely before cutting into slices.

blueberry muffins

A simple and delicious 'wet and dry' muffin recipe.

Preparation time: 15 minutes
Servings: About 12 muffins

....

dry
2 cups SR flour
¾ cup caster sugar
1 teaspoon baking powder

wet
½ cup vegetable oil
1 cup soy milk
½ teaspoon vanilla essence
1 cup blueberries (fresh or frozen)

....

Preheat oven to 180°C and grease and line a 12-hole muffin tray with paper cases.

1. Mix dry ingredients in a large bowl.
2. Make a well in centre of dry ingredients and add wet ingredients.
3. Mix together until they form a batter (not too much mixing).
4. Add blueberries and stir (if using frozen berries, run them under cold water to thaw slightly before adding).
5. Spoon into prepared muffin pan, filling close to the top of each case.
6. Bake for 15–20 minutes or until a skewer inserted into muffin comes out clean.
7. Cool in muffin tray for 5 minutes before turning out onto wire rack.

orange muffins

These are delicious and sweet.

Preparation time: 15 minutes
Servings: About 10 muffins

....

dry 1½ cups SR flour
2⁄3 cup caster sugar
1 teaspoon baking powder

wet 1⁄3 cup vegetable oil
2⁄3 cup orange juice

....

Preheat oven to 180°C and grease and line a 12-hole muffin tray with paper cases.

1. Mix dry ingredients in a large bowl.
2. Make a well in centre of dry ingredients and add wet ingredients.
3. Mix together until they form a batter (not too much mixing).
4. Spoon into prepared muffin pan, filling close to the top of each case.
5. Bake for 15–20 minutes or until a skewer inserted into muffin comes out clean.
6. Cool in muffin tray for 5 minutes before turning out onto wire rack.

apple and cinnamon muffins

Preparation time: 15 minutes
Servings: About 12 muffins

 dry
2 cups SR flour
½ cup caster sugar
2 teaspoons cinnamon

wet
1 cup tinned baking apples, mashed lightly
1 teaspoon vanilla essence
1 cup soy milk
½ cup vegetable oil

Preheat oven to 180°C and grease or line a 12-hole muffin tray with paper cases.

1. Mix dry ingredients in a large bowl.
2. Make a well in centre of dry ingredients and add wet ingredients.
3. Mix together until they form a batter (not too much mixing).
4. Spoon into prepared muffin pan, filling close to the top of each case.
5. Bake for 20–25 minutes or until a skewer inserted into muffin comes out clean.
6. Cool in tray for 5 minutes before turning out onto wire rack.

apricot and choc-chip muffins

Preparation time: 15 minutes
Servings: About 12 muffins

dry 1½ cups SR flour
½ cups caster sugar
¼ cup cocoa
½ cup dairy-free, nut-free chocolate chips
½ cup dried apricots, chopped

wet ½ cup vegetable oil
1 cup apricot nectar

Preheat oven to 180°C and grease or line a 12-hole muffin tray with paper cases.

1. Mix dry ingredients in a large bowl.
2. Make a well in centre of dry ingredients and add wet ingredients.
3. Mix together until they form a batter (not too much mixing).
4. Spoon into prepared muffin pan, filling close to the top of each case.
5. Bake for 20–25 minutes or until a skewer inserted into muffin comes out clean.
6. Cool in tray for 5 minutes before turning out onto wire rack.

banana and choc-chip muffins

A delicious combination.

Preparation time: 15 minutes
Servings: About 12 muffins

 1½ cups SR flour
½ cup caster sugar
1 teaspoon baking powder
2 tablespoons cocoa
¼ cup dairy-free, nut-free chocolate chips

 ½ cup ripe bananas, mashed (about 2 small bananas)
½ cup vegetable oil
¾ cup soy milk

Preheat oven to 180°C and grease or line a 12-hole muffin tray with paper cases.

1. Mix dry ingredients in a large bowl.
2. Make a well in centre of dry ingredients and add wet ingredients.
3. Mix together until they form a batter (not too much mixing).
4. Spoon into prepared muffin pan, filling close to the top of each case.
5. Bake for 15–20 minutes or until a skewer inserted into muffin comes out clean.
6. Cool in tray for 5 minutes before turning out onto wire rack.

crazy craisin muffins

The sweet dried cranberries give these muffins a lovely subtle flavour kids love.

Preparation time: 15 minutes
Servings: About 12 muffins

dry 2 cups SR flour
½ cup caster sugar
½ cup craisins

wet ¼ cup vegetable oil
1 teaspoon vanilla essence
¾ cup soy milk

Preheat oven to 180°C and grease or line a 12-hole muffin tray with paper cases.

1. Mix dry ingredients in a large bowl.
2. Make a well in centre of dry ingredients and add wet ingredients.
3. Mix together until they form a batter (not too much mixing).
4. Spoon into prepared muffin pan, filling close to the top of each case.
5. Bake for 15–20 minutes or until a skewer inserted into muffin comes out clean.
6. Cool in muffin trays for 5 minutes before turning out onto wire rack.

banana
bread

This is great toasted for breakfast with a little dairy-free spread.

Preparation time: 15 minutes

2 cups SR flour (or gluten-free SR flour)
½ cup sugar
1 teaspoon cinnamon (plus extra)
2 cups ripe banana, mashed (about 6 medium bananas)
1 teaspoon vanilla essence
Brown sugar

Preheat oven to 180°C and grease and line a 23 cm x 13 cm loaf tin with non-stick baking paper.

1. Combine flour, sugar and cinnamon together in a large bowl and mix well.
2. Make a well in centre of dry ingredients and add mashed banana and vanilla.
3. Mix together until they form a thick batter.
4. Spread into prepared tin and sprinkle top with brown sugar and extra cinnamon.
5. Bake for 50–60 minutes or until a skewer inserted into loaf comes out clean.
6. Cool in loaf tin for 10 minutes before turning out onto wire rack.

easiest coconut fruit loaf

Preparation time: 10 minutes

1 cup SR flour
1 cup brown sugar
1 cup desiccated coconut
1 cup sultanas
1 cup soy milk

Preheat oven to 180°C and grease and line a 23 cm x 13 cm loaf tin with non-stick baking paper.

1. Mix dry ingredients in a large bowl.
2. Make a well in centre of dry ingredients and pour in soy milk.
3. Mix together until they form a batter (not too much mixing).
4. Pour into prepared loaf tin and bake for 30–40 minutes or until a skewer inserted into loaf comes out clean.
5. Cool in loaf tin for 10 minutes before turning out onto wire rack.

fruity loaf

A great-tasting loaf with extra hidden fibre.

Preparation time: 15 minutes

....

1 cup All-Bran cereal
1 cup mixed dried fruit
1½ cups soy milk
1 cup SR flour

....

Preheat oven to 180°C and grease and line a 23 cm x 13 cm loaf tin with non-stick baking paper.

1. Combine All-Bran, dried fruit and soy milk in a large bowl. Let rest for 10 minutes.
2. Add flour and mix well with a large metal spoon.
3. Spoon mixture into loaf tin and bake for 30–35 minutes or until a skewer inserted into loaf comes out clean.
4. Leave to cool in tin for 10 minutes then turn out onto wire rack.

date and oat loaf

This loaf is delicious when served warm with some dairy-free spread. It is best eaten on the day it's made.

Preparation time: 15 minutes

1 cup dates, chopped
2 tablespoons golden syrup
1 cup boiling water
1 ¼ cups plain flour
1 teaspoon bicarbonate of soda
½ cup brown sugar
¾ cup rolled oats

Preheat oven to 180°C and grease and line a 23 cm x 13 cm loaf tin with non-stick baking paper.

1. Combine dates, golden syrup and boiling water in a large bowl and mix together. Let rest for 10 minutes.
2. Add flour, bicarbonate of soda, sugar and oats to date mixture and stir until well combined.
3. Pour into prepared loaf tin and bake for 35–40 minutes or until a skewer inserted into loaf comes out clean.
4. Cool in tin for 10 minutes before turning out onto wire rack.

jam tarts

All the kids love these. Pastry sheets made without egg or milk can be found at most large supermarkets.

Preparation time: 15 minutes
Servings: 18 tarts

2 sheets vegan shortcrust or puff pastry sheets, thawed
½ cup strawberry jam

Preheat oven to 200°C and grease two 12-hole muffin trays.

1. Use a circle cutter (approx. 7 cm) to cut 9 circles from each sheet of pastry.
2. Press pastry circles into greased muffin holes.
3. Spoon teaspoons of jam into each pastry.
4. Bake for 10–15 minutes or until pastry is lightly golden.
5. Cool in trays for 5 minutes before turning out onto wire rack.

white chocolate bites

Preparation time: 15 minutes
Servings: About 15 pieces

1½ cups (about 200 g) dairy-free, nut-free white chocolate
¼ cup Nuttelex (or other dairy-free spread)
3 cups rice bubbles (or gluten-free rice bubbles)
¼ cup golden syrup
½ cup mini marshmallows (or gluten-free mini marshmallows)

Line baking tray with non-stick baking paper and assemble 15 paper cases on top.

1. Break the chocolate into small pieces and place in medium heatproof bowl with Nuttelex.
2. Microwave on high for 1 minute. Stir well to combine. If not quite melted, heat for further intervals of 30 seconds on high until completely melted.
3. Add rice bubbles, golden syrup and chopped marshmallows to melted chocolate mix. Stir to combine well.
4. Drop spoonfuls of mixture into paper cases and refrigerate until set.

one bowl
and *plus a saucepan*
20 minutes

In this section . . .

cinnamon cookies

Crunchy cookies with a delicate cinnamon flavour.

Preparation time: 20 minutes
Servings: About 18 cookies

....

½ cup Nuttelex (or other dairy-free spread)
1 tablespoon golden syrup
2 tablespoons soy milk
1 cup wholemeal plain flour
⅓ cup sugar
⅔ cup rolled oats
1 teaspoon cinnamon
½ teaspoon bicarbonate of soda

....

Preheat oven to 180°C and grease or line biscuit trays with non-stick baking paper.

1. Stir Nuttelex, golden syrup and soy milk in a small saucepan over low heat until melted and combined.
2. Place remaining ingredients in a large bowl and combine well.
3. Stir melted mixture into dry ingredients and mix well.
4. Roll teaspoons of mixture into balls and place on prepared trays. Flatten slightly with a fork.
5. Bake for 10–15 minutes or until lightly browned.
6. Remove from oven and cool slightly on trays before placing on wire racks to cool.

anzac biscuits

A classic Australian favourite.

Preparation time: 20 minutes
Servings: About 25 biscuits

....

½ cup Nuttelex (or other dairy-free spread)
2 tablespoons golden syrup
1 teaspoon bicarbonate of soda
2 tablespoons boiling water
1 cup rolled oats
1 cup plain flour
1 cup caster sugar
¾ cup desiccated coconut

....

Preheat oven to 150°C and grease or line biscuit trays with non-stick baking paper.

1. Stir Nuttelex and golden syrup in a small saucepan over low heat until melted and combined.
2. Dissolve bicarbonate of soda in boiling water and add to melted mixture.
3. Place oats, flour, sugar and coconut in a large bowl and combine well.
4. Stir melted mixture into dry ingredients and mix well.
5. Roll teaspoons of mixture into balls and place on prepared trays, allowing room for spreading. Flatten slightly with a fork.
6. Bake for 8–10 minutes or until golden brown.
7. Remove from oven and cool slightly on trays before placing on wire racks to cool.

ginger snaps

Preparation time: 20 minutes
Servings: About 40 biscuits

....

½ cup Nuttelex (or other dairy-free spread)
¾ cup golden syrup
2 cups SR flour
I tablespoon ground ginger
¼ teaspoon nutmeg
½ cup brown sugar

....

Preheat oven to 160°C and grease or line biscuit trays with non-stick baking paper.

1. Stir Nuttelex and golden syrup in a medium saucepan and stir over low heat until melted and combined. Remove to cool slightly.
2. Place remaining ingredients in a large bowl and combine well.
3. Stir melted mixture into dry ingredients and mix well. Let stand for 5 minutes.
4. Place rounded teaspoons of mixture on baking trays, allowing room for spreading. Flatten slightly with a fork.
5. Bake for 15 minutes or until golden brown.
6. Remove from oven and cool slightly on trays before placing on wire racks to cool.

oat crunch cookies

Preparation time: 20 minutes
Servings: About 30 cookies

½ cup Nuttelex (or other dairy-free spread)
1 tablespoon honey
2 tablespoons water
1 cup wholemeal SR flour
1 cup raw sugar
1 cup rolled oats
1 cup desiccated coconut

Preheat oven to 180°C and grease or line biscuit trays with non-stick baking paper.

1. Stir Nuttelex, honey and water in a small saucepan over low heat until melted and combined.
2. Place flour, sugar, oats and coconut in a large bowl and mix well.
3. Stir melted mixture into dry ingredients and combine well.
4. Place rounded spoonfuls of mixture on trays, using fingers to press mounds together. Flatten slightly as they will not spread much.
5. Bake for 10–12 minutes or until golden brown.
6. Remove from oven and cool slightly on trays before placing on wire racks to cool.

chocolate hedgehog

A classic recipe the whole family will enjoy. These are best stored in an airtight container in the refrigerator.

Preparation time: 20 minutes
Servings: About 25 squares

....

¼ cup Nuttelex (or other dairy-free spread)
2 tablespoons honey
1½ cups (about 200 g) dairy-free, nut-free chocolate pieces
2½ cups (about 250 g) dairy-free, nut-free, egg-free (and gluten-free) plain sweet biscuits
Sprinkles (or gluten-free sprinkles)

....

Prepare a 20 cm square baking tray by greasing and lining with non-stick baking paper.

1. Stir Nuttelex, honey and chocolate in a medium saucepan over low heat until melted and combined.
2. Finely crush biscuits by placing in a plastic snap-lock bag and rolling with rolling pin.
3. Stir crushed biscuits into chocolate mixture and combine well.
4. Spread mix into prepared tray using back of metal spoon. Decorate with sprinkles.
5. Refrigerate until set then cut into squares.

chocolate bubble bars

Store these in an airtight container in the refrigerator.

Preparation time: 15 minutes
Servings: About 16 bars or 20 squares

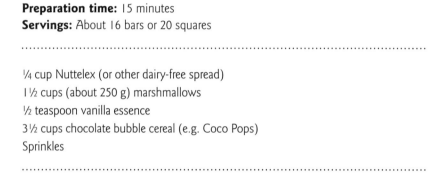

¼ cup Nuttelex (or other dairy-free spread)
1½ cups (about 250 g) marshmallows
½ teaspoon vanilla essence
3½ cups chocolate bubble cereal (e.g. Coco Pops)
Sprinkles

Prepare a 20 cm square baking tray by greasing and lining with non-stick baking paper.

1. Stir Nuttelex and marshmallows in a medium saucepan over low heat until smooth and combined.
2. Remove from heat and stir in vanilla essence.
3. Place bubble cereal in a large bowl.
4. Pour marshmallow mix into bowl of bubble cereal and work quickly to mix.
5. Press firmly into prepared tray using back of metal spoon or wet clean hands if necessary. Shake sprinkles over top.
6. Refrigerate for a few hours until set then cut into squares or bars.

crunchy chocolate squares

A lovely chocolate slice with a bit of crunch, best stored in an airtight container in the refrigerator.

Preparation time: 15 minutes
Servings: About 25 squares

¼ cup Nuttelex (or other dairy-free spread)
¾ cup (about 100 g) dairy-free, nut-free chocolate
2 tablespoons golden syrup
3 cups cornflakes (or gluten-free cornflakes)
⅓ cup desiccated coconut

Prepare a 20 cm square baking tray by greasing and lining with non-stick baking paper.

1. Stir Nuttelex, chocolate and golden syrup in a small saucepan over low heat until melted and combined.
2. Place the cornflakes in a large bowl and crush lightly. Stir in coconut.
3. Stir melted mixture into dry ingredients and combine well.
4. Press firmly into prepared tray using back of metal spoon.
5. Refrigerate until set then cut into squares.

mallow crunch

These are best stored in an airtight container in the refrigerator.

Preparation time: 15 minutes
Servings: About 20 pieces

¼ cup Nuttelex (or other dairy-free spread)
1½ cup marshmallows (or gluten-free marshmallows)
3 cups cornflakes (or gluten-free cornflakes)
½ cup chopped dried fruit (e.g. apricots, peaches, pears, sultanas)

Prepare a 20 cm square baking tray by greasing and lining with non-stick baking paper.

1. Stir Nuttelex and marshmallows in a medium saucepan over low heat until melted, smooth and combined.
2. Combine cornflakes and dried fruit in a large bowl.
3. Pour melted mixture over cereal and work fast to combine well.
4. Press firmly into prepared tray using back of metal spoon or wet clean hands.
5. Refrigerate until firm then cut into slices.

golden oat slice

A tasty chewy slice.

Preparation time: 15 minutes
Servings: About 20 pieces

....

½ cup Nuttelex (or other dairy-free spread)
¼ cup golden syrup
½ cup brown sugar
2¾ cups rolled oats (or gluten-free rolled oats)

....

Preheat oven to 180°C and grease and line a 20 cm square baking tray with non-stick baking paper.

1. Stir Nuttelex, golden syrup and sugar in a medium saucepan over low heat until melted and combined.
2. Stir in the oats and combine well.
3. Press into prepared tray using back of metal spoon or wet clean hands.
4. Bake for 15–20 minutes or until golden brown.
5. Allow to cool in tray for 10 minutes then cut into pieces while still warm. Cool completely before removing from tray.

sunflower slice

Kids love eating the sunflower seeds in this slice.

Preparation time: 15 minutes
Servings: About 25 squares

....

½ cup Nuttelex (or other dairy-free spread)
¾ cup honey
5 cups cornflakes (or gluten-free cornflakes)
⅓ cup sunflower seeds
⅓ cup desiccated coconut
⅓ cup glace cherries, chopped

....

Prepare a 20 cm square tray by greasing and lining with non-stick baking paper.

1. Stir Nuttelex and honey in a small saucepan over low heat until melted and combined.
2. Increase heat until boiling then reduce to a simmer for 5 minutes.
3. Place the cornflakes in a large bowl and crush lightly. Stir in remaining ingredients.
4. Stir melted mixture into dry ingredients and combine well.
5. Spread mix into prepared tray using back of metal spoon.
6. Refrigerate until set then cut into squares.

honey
fruit bars

These are a great addition to the school lunchbox.

Preparation time: 20 minutes
Servings: About 18 bars

1 cup Nuttelex (or other dairy-free spread)
1 tablespoon honey
1 cup raw sugar
2½ cups mixed dried fruit
1½ cups SR flour (or gluten-free SR flour)
1 cup coconut
1 cup natural bran (or gluten-free bran)

Preheat oven to 160°C and grease a 24 cm x 30 cm lamington tray or line with non-stick baking paper.

1. Stir Nuttelex, honey, sugar and fruit in a medium saucepan over low heat until melted and combined.
2. Combine flour, coconut and bran in a large bowl and mix well.
3. Stir melted mixture into dry ingredients and combine well.
4. Press mixture into tray and bake for 20–25 minutes or until golden brown.
5. Allow to cool completely in tray then cut into bars.

sultana loaf

A delicious loaf; try it toasted with dairy-free spread.

Preparation time: 15 minutes

....

1 tablespoon Nuttelex (or other dairy-free spread)
1 cup sultanas
1 cup sugar
1 cup water
2 cups SR flour

....

Preheat oven to 180°C and grease and line a 23 cm x 13 cm loaf tin with non-stick baking paper.

1. Stir Nuttelex, sultanas, sugar and water in a medium saucepan over heat until boiling then reduce heat and simmer for 5 minutes.
2. Pour into mixing bowl to cool slightly (place in refrigerator to speed cooling).
3. Add flour to cooled mixture and combine well.
4. Bake for 40–45 minutes or until a skewer inserted into loaf comes out clean.
5. Cool in cake tin for 10 minutes before turning out onto wire rack.

chocolate bubble bites

For all little kids – and big. Don't forget to store in an airtight container in the refrigerator.

Preparation time: 20 minutes
Servings: About 25 crackles

250 g copha, melted
4 cups rice bubbles (or gluten-free rice bubbles)
1 cup icing sugar (or gluten-free icing sugar)
¼ cup cocoa
1 cup desiccated coconut
Sprinkles (or gluten-free sprinkles)

Line baking tray with non-stick baking paper and assemble 25 paper cases on top.

1. Melt copha in a medium saucepan over gentle heat.
2. Combine all other ingredients in a large bowl and mix together.
3. Add melted copha to dry ingredients and mix well.
4. Spoon mixture into paper cases and decorate with sprinkles.
5. Refrigerate until set.

chocolate crunchies

A very easy, sweet treat, best stored in an airtight container in the refrigerator, and great for parties.

Preparation time: 20 minutes
Servings: About 12 chocolates

....

1 cup rice bubbles (or gluten-free rice bubbles)
¾ cup (about 100 g) dairy-free, nut-free chocolate
1½ teaspoons Nuttelex (or other dairy-free spread)
Sprinkles (or gluten-free sprinkles)

....

Line baking tray with non-stick baking paper and assemble 12 paper cases on top.

1. Place rice bubbles in a small saucepan and stir over medium heat until lightly toasted. Remove from heat.
2. Break the chocolate into small pieces and place in medium heatproof bowl with Nuttelex.
3. Microwave on high for 1 minute. Stir well to combine. If not quite melted, heat for further intervals of 30 seconds on high until completely melted.
4. Add chocolate mixture to rice bubbles.
5. Spoon mixture into paper cases and decorate with sprinkles.
6. Refrigerate until set.

chocolate bran bites

These are best stored in an airtight container in the refrigerator.

Preparation time: 20 minutes
Servings: About 15 pieces

....

2 tablespoons Nuttelex (or other dairy-free spread)
2 tablespoons honey
½ cup (about 70 g) dairy-free, nut-free chocolate pieces
2½ cups Sultana Bran

....

Line baking tray with non-stick baking paper and assemble 15 paper cases on top.

1. Stir Nuttelex, honey and chocolate in a medium saucepan over low heat until melted and combined.
2. Add the Sultana Bran and combine well.
3. Spoon mixture into paper cases and place in refrigerator to set.

honey jumbles

Preparation time: 20 minutes
Servings: About 18 pieces

....

3 tablespoons Nuttelex (or other dairy-free spread)
1 tablespoon honey
2 tablespoons caster sugar
3 cups cornflakes (or gluten-free cornflakes)

....

Preheat oven to 170°C and place 18 paper cases in two 12-hole muffin trays.

1. Stir Nuttelex, honey and sugar in a small saucepan over low heat until sugar is dissolved and colour changes.
2. Place cornflakes in a large bowl, add melted mixture and combine well.
3. Spoon mixture into paper cases.
4. Bake for 10 minutes or until starting to brown.
5. Cool in tray for 5 minutes before turning out onto wire rack.

one bowl
and
30 minutes

In this section . . .

melt in your mouth moments

gluten free option

Try not to eat all of these yourself. If making with gluten-free flour, flatten well as they will not spread as much.

Preparation time: 20 minutes
Servings: About 20 biscuits, 10 sandwiched together

....

½ cup Nuttelex (or other dairy-free spread)
½ teaspoon vanilla essence
¼ cup icing sugar
½ cup cornflour
½ cup plain flour (or gluten-free plain flour)
¼ cup SR flour (or gluten-free SR flour)

....

Preheat oven to 180°C and grease or line biscuit trays with non-stick baking paper.

1. Mix Nuttelex, vanilla and sugar together in a large bowl with a large metal spoon until well combined (use back of spoon to push mix together).
2. Stir in flours and mix well. If mixture is too sticky, add a little extra plain flour.
3. Roll teaspoons of mixture into balls and place on baking trays, allowing room for spreading. Flatten slightly with a fork.
4. Bake for 12–15 minutes or until the biscuits are lightly golden.
5. Remove from oven and cool slightly on trays before placing on wire racks to cool.
6. Once cool, sandwich biscuits together with your choice of orange-cream icing (see p. 120) or chocolate-cream icing (see p. 119). Alternatively, these are delicious when joined together with jam or dairy-free, nut-free chocolate spread.

gingerbread biscuit shapes

Don't be daunted by the number of ingredients, it is still a simple one bowl recipe and the biscuits are delicious.

Preparation time: 30 minutes
Servings: About 12 large or 24 small shapes

....

½ cup Nuttelex (or other dairy-free spread)
½ cup brown sugar
2 tablespoons water
2 tablespoons golden syrup
2 tablespoons molasses
1 teaspoon cinnamon
1 teaspoon ground ginger
1 tablespoon cocoa
2½ cups SR flour

....

Preheat oven to 180°C and grease or line biscuit trays with non-stick baking paper.

1. Mix Nuttelex and brown sugar together in a large bowl with large metal spoon until well combined (use back of spoon to push mix together).
2. Add water, golden syrup and molasses and combine well.
3. Stir in spices and cocoa.
4. Add flour in batches and mix to a dough using clean hands if needed.

5. Place dough onto floured board and knead until smooth (if dry add a small amount of water; if sticky add small amounts of flour).
6. Roll dough to about 5 mm thick and use cutters to cut into any shapes you like. Keep rolling out dough until all is used.
7. Place shapes onto prepared trays and bake for 10–12 minutes or until the edges start to brown.
8. Remove from oven and cool slightly on trays before placing on wire racks to cool.
9. Once cool, decorate as desired.

chocolate orange cookies

A lovely combination of flavours.

Preparation time: 30 minutes
Servings: About 30 cookies

....

½ cup Nuttelex (or other dairy-free spread)
¼ cup caster sugar
½ cup brown sugar
½ teaspoon vanilla essence
3 tablespoons orange juice
1½ teaspoons orange rind, finely grated
2 cups SR flour
½ cup dairy-free, nut-free chocolate chips

....

Preheat oven to 180°C and grease or line biscuit trays with non-stick baking paper.

1. Mix Nuttelex and sugars together in a large bowl with a large metal spoon until well combined (use back of spoon to push mix together).
2. Add vanilla, orange juice and orange rind and mix well.
3. Add flour and chocolate chips and mix until well combined.
4. Roll teaspoons of mix into balls and place on baking trays, allowing room for spreading. Flatten a little with a fork
5. Bake for 10–12 minutes or until golden brown.
6. Remove from oven and cool slightly on trays before placing on wire racks to cool.

shortbread biscuits

These rich buttery biscuits are easy to make.

Preparation time: 30 minutes
Servings: About 20 medium biscuits

....

2 cups plain flour
1 tablespoon rice flour
¼ cup icing sugar
¾ cup Nuttelex (or other dairy-free spread), straight from fridge

....

Preheat oven to 180°C and grease or line biscuit trays with non-stick baking paper.

1. Mix flours and sugar in a large bowl.
2. Cut cold Nuttelex into small pieces and rub into flour mixture with fingertips until it resembles fine breadcrumbs and no large pieces of Nuttelex remain.
3. Place dough onto floured board and knead lightly until smooth (if dry add a small amount of water; if sticky add small amounts of flour).
4. Roll out to 5 mm thick and cut into any shapes desired.
5. Place shapes onto prepared trays and bake for 15–20 minutes or until a pale golden colour.
6. Remove from oven and cool slightly on trays before placing on wire racks to cool.

orange shortbread biscuits

A delicious biscuit with a tangy citrus flavour.

Preparation time: 30 minutes
Servings: About 16 biscuits

....

½ cup Nuttelex (or other dairy-free spread)
2 tablespoons caster sugar
1⅓ cup plain flour
½ teaspoon mixed spice
2 tablespoons soy milk
⅓ cup currants
2 teaspoons lemon rind, finely grated
2 teaspoons orange rind, finely grated

....

Preheat oven to 180°C and grease or line biscuit trays with non-stick baking paper.

1. Mix Nuttelex and sugar together in a large bowl with a large metal spoon until well combined (use back of spoon to push mix together).
2. Stir in flour and spice and mix well.
3. Add soy milk and mix to form a dough.
4. Lightly combine currants and rinds into dough.
5. Turn out onto a lightly floured surface and gently knead until smooth. Use a lightly floured rolling pin to roll dough out to 5 mm thick. Cut out shapes with cutters.
6. Place on prepared trays and bake for 10–12 minutes or until the biscuits start to brown at the edges.
7. Remove from oven and cool slightly on trays before placing on wire racks to cool.

viennese fingers

It's worthwhile making the effort to sandwich these with jam and dip in chocolate.

Preparation time: 30 minutes
Servings: About 24 biscuits, 12 sandwiched together

....

1 cup Nuttelex (or other dairy-free spread)
¼ cup caster sugar
2 cups plain flour
1 teaspoon vanilla essence

....

Preheat oven to 180°C and grease or line biscuit trays with non-stick baking paper.

1. Mix together Nuttelex and sugar in a large bowl with a large metal spoon until well combined (use back of spoon to push mix together).
2. Add flour and vanilla and combine well.
3. Put mix into a piping bag fitted with a large star shape nozzle. Pipe finger length amounts onto prepared baking tray.
4. Bake for 12–15 minutes or until the biscuits are lightly golden.
5. Remove from oven and cool slightly on trays before placing on wire racks to cool.
6. For a traditional finish, sandwich two biscuits together with jam and then dip half of each biscuit in melted dairy-free, nut-free chocolate. Chocolate can be melted by breaking into small pieces and placing in heatproof bowl in microwave for 1 minute on high. Stir well and if needed, heat again in intervals of 30 seconds on high until completely melted.

oatmeal cookies

A crunchy wholemeal biscuit.

Preparation time: 30 minutes
Servings: About 18 cookies

¾ cup SR flour
¾ cup wholemeal plain flour
½ cup rolled oats
½ teaspoon mixed spice
½ cup Nuttelex (or other dairy-free spread), straight from fridge
½ cup brown sugar
2 tablespoons soy milk

Preheat oven to 190°C and grease or line biscuit trays with non-stick baking paper.

1. Mix flours, rolled oats and spice in a large bowl.
2. Cut cold Nuttelex into small pieces and rub into flour mixture with fingertips until it resembles breadcrumbs and no large pieces of Nuttelex remain.
3. Add brown sugar to mixture and combine well.
4. Add soy milk to mixture and use clean hands to mix to a firm dough (add more milk if dough is too dry).
5. Use a lightly floured rolling pin to roll dough out to about 5 mm thick. Dip cutters in flour to cut out desired shapes.
6. Place on a tray and bake for 8–10 minutes or until golden brown.
7. Remove from oven and cool slightly on trays before placing on wire racks to cool.

rock cakes

These are delicious served for afternoon tea.

Preparation time: 30 minutes
Servings: About 12 cakes

- -

1 cup SR flour
½ teaspoon mixed spice
1 teaspoon baking powder
½ cup Nuttelex (or other dairy-free spread), straight from fridge
¼ cup caster sugar (plus extra)
⅔ cup sultanas
3 tablespoons soy milk

- -

Preheat oven to 180°C and grease or line biscuit trays with non-stick baking paper.

1. Mix flour, mixed spice and baking powder in a large bowl.
2. Cut cold Nuttelex into small pieces and rub into flour mixture with fingertips until it resembles fine breadcrumbs and no large pieces of Nuttelex remain.
3. Add sugar and sultanas to mixture and combine well.
4. Make a well in the centre of the mixture and pour in the soy milk. Use a round-bladed knife to mix together using a cutting motion to make a soft dough.
5. Spoon mixture out in rough heaps on prepared trays and sprinkle with extra sugar.
6. Bake for 12–15 minutes or until golden brown.
7. Remove from oven and cool slightly on trays before placing on wire racks to cool.

fruit scrolls

When served warm for breakfast these are hard to resist.

Preparation time: 30 minutes
Servings: About 12 scrolls

....

2 cups SR flour
1 tablespoon Nuttelex (or other dairy-free spread), straight from fridge,
    plus 2 extra tablespoons
¾ cup soy milk
⅓ cup mixed dried fruit
¼ cup caster sugar (plus extra)
½ teaspoon cinnamon

....

Preheat oven to 190°C and grease or line biscuit tray with non-stick baking paper.

1. Place flour into large bowl. Cut cold Nuttelex into small pieces and rub into flour mixture with fingertips until it resembles fine breadcrumbs and no large pieces of Nuttelex remain.
2. Make a well in the centre of the mix and pour in the soy milk. Use a round-bladed knife to mix together using a cutting motion to make a soft dough.
3. Turn out onto a lightly floured surface and gently knead until smooth.

4. Use a lightly floured rolling pin to roll dough out to a 30 cm x 20 cm shape.
5. Spread with extra Nuttelex then sprinkle fruit, sugar and cinnamon over centre.
6. Roll up dough from long side and cut into 12 slices. Place closely together on tray.
7. Sprinkle tops with extra sugar and bake for 15–20 minutes or until golden.
8. Remove from oven and cool slightly on trays before placing on wire racks to cool.

scones

A dairy-free recipe for traditional scones.

Preparation time: 30 minutes
Servings: About 12 scones

....

2 cups SR flour
Pinch of salt
2 tablespoons icing sugar
⅓ cup Nuttelex, straight from fridge
½ cup soy milk

....

Preheat oven to 220°C and grease or line biscuit tray with non-stick baking paper.

1. Mix flour, salt and sugar together in a large bowl.
2. Cut cold Nuttelex into small pieces and rub into flour mixture with fingertips until it resembles fine breadcrumbs and no large pieces of Nuttelex remain.
3. Make a well in the centre of the mixture and pour in the soy milk. Use a round-bladed knife to mix together using a cutting motion to make a soft dough.
4. Once the mix holds together, turn out onto a lightly floured surface and gently knead until smooth.
5. Use a lightly floured rolling pin to roll dough out to about 2 cm thick. Dip 5 cm diameter cutter in flour to cut out scone shapes.
6. Place scones on a tray and brush tops with extra soy milk (or use clean fingers if brush has been used for butter previously).
7. Bake for 10–12 minutes or until golden and scones sound hollow when tapped.

banana and date scones

Absolutely delicious!

Preparation time: 30 minutes
Servings: About 12 scones

....

2 cups SR flour
¼ teaspoon mixed spice
¼ teaspoon cinnamon
1 cup dates, chopped
1 teaspoon lemon rind, finely grated
1 small banana, mashed
¾ cup soy milk
1 teaspoon lemon juice

....

Preheat oven to 220°C and grease or line biscuit tray with non-stick baking paper.

1. Mix flour and spices in a large bowl.
2. Add dates and lemon rind and combine well.
3. Make a well in the centre of dry ingredients and add banana, milk and lemon juice. Use a round-bladed knife to mix together using a cutting motion to make a soft dough.
4. Turn dough out onto a lightly floured surface and gently knead until smooth.
5. Use a lightly floured rolling pin to roll dough out to about 2 cm thick. Dip 5 cm diameter cutter in flour before cutting out scone shapes.
6. Place scones on a tray and brush tops with extra soy milk (or use clean fingers if brush has been used for butter previously).
7. Bake for 12–15 minutes or until golden and scones sound hollow when tapped.

one bowl
and *plus a saucepan*
30 minutes

In this section . . .

mum's biscuits

My kids love helping to make these biscuits, especially when they can add any filling they like. Let your imagination go wild!

Preparation time: 30 minutes
Servings: About 60 biscuits

2¼ cups (500 g) Nuttelex (or other dairy-free spread)
1 quantity sweetened condensed soy milk (see pages 113 and 114)
1 cup sugar
5 cups SR flour
Choice of flavourings such as jam, choc chips, sprinkles (see below)

Preheat oven to 180°C and grease or line biscuit trays with non-stick baking paper.

1. Mix Nuttelex and sugar together in a large bowl with a large metal spoon until well combined (use back of spoon to push mix together).
2. Add sweetened condensed soy milk and mix well.
3. Add flour in two batches and carefully combine. Use the back of a spoon to push flour into mix.
4. Add your choice of ingredients to create different flavoured biscuits. For example chocolate chips, sultanas/cornflakes, rice bubbles/coconut, sprinkles or use your finger to make an indent for jam.
5. Roll teaspoons of mixture into balls and place on prepared trays. Flatten slightly with a fork.
6. Bake for 10–15 minutes or until golden brown.
7. Remove from oven and cool slightly on trays before placing on wire racks to cool.

florentines

This no-nut version tastes delicious.

Preparation time: 30 minutes
Servings: About 24 biscuits

2 cups cornflakes, crushed (or gluten-free cornflakes)
¾ cup sultanas
½ cup glace cherries, chopped
⅔ cup sweetened condensed soy milk (see pages 113 and 114)
¾ cup (about 100 g) dairy-free, nut-free chocolate pieces

Preheat oven to 180°C and grease or line biscuit trays with non-stick baking paper.

1. Combine cornflakes, sultanas, cherries and sweetened condensed soy milk in a large bowl and mix together. Press mixture together using back of spoon.
2. Place spoonfuls of mixture in heaps on trays.
3. Bake for 12–15 minutes or until lightly golden.
4. Remove from oven and cool slightly on trays before placing on wire racks to cool.
5. Once biscuits are cold, melt chocolate by placing small pieces in heatproof bowl in microwave for 1 minute on high. Stir well and, if needed, heat again in intervals of 30 seconds on high until completely melted.
6. Spread chocolate over base of each biscuit.
7. Once chocolate is set, store in an airtight container in the refrigerator.

coconut macaroons

These biscuits are best eaten on the day they're baked or they will soften.

Preparation time: 30 minutes
Servings: About 24 biscuits

....

3½ cups shredded coconut
1 quantity sweetened condensed soy milk (see pages 113 and 114)
2 teaspoons vanilla essence

....

Preheat oven to 170°C and grease or line biscuit trays with non-stick baking paper.

1. Combine all ingredients in a large bowl and mix together.
2. Use wet clean hands or spoon to put small mounds on baking tray. Flatten slightly as they will not spread much.
3. Bake for 10–12 minutes or until lightly browned.
4. Remove from oven and cool slightly on trays before placing on wire racks to cool.

chocolate caramel slice

A delicious slice that no one believes is allergy-free.

Preparation time: 30 minutes
Servings: About 25 squares

....

1 cup SR flour
1 cup rolled oats
½ cup brown sugar
1 cup desiccated coconut
⅔ cup Nuttelex (or other dairy-free spread), melted, plus 1 extra tablespoon
1 quantity sweetened condensed soy milk (see pages 113 and 114)
2 tablespoons golden syrup
1½ cups (about 200 g) dairy-free, nut-free chocolate, melted

....

Preheat oven to 180°C and grease and line a 20 cm square baking tray with non-stick baking paper.

1. Mix flour, oats, sugar, coconut and melted Nuttelex in a large bowl. Press into base of prepared tray using back of spoon.
2. Bake for 12–15 minutes or until golden brown.
3. In a small saucepan, combine sweetened condensed soy milk, golden syrup and extra Nuttelex. Bring to boil over a low heat, stirring constantly until a light caramel colour. Remove from heat.

4. Pour caramel carefully over cooked base and spread evenly.
5. Return to oven and bake a further 12 minutes. Cool in tray.
6. Once cooled, spread melted chocolate over caramel filling. To melt chocolate, break the chocolate into small pieces and place in small heatproof bowl. Microwave on high for 1 minute. Stir well to combine. If not quite melted, heat for further intervals of 30 seconds on high until completely melted.
7. Allow to cool completely in refrigerator before cutting into squares to serve.

lemon slice

This delicious tangy coconut slice is best stored in an airtight container in the fridge. It also freezes well when wrapped tightly in cling wrap. Thaw at room temperature for about 30 minutes prior to serving.

Preparation time: 30 minutes
Servings: About 25 pieces

⅓ cup Nuttelex (or other dairy-free spread)
1 quantity sweetened condensed soy milk (see pages 113 and 114)
1 tablespoon fresh lemon juice
2½ cups (about 250 g) dairy-free, nut-free, egg-free (and gluten-free)
    plain sweet biscuits
1 cup desiccated coconut (plus extra)

Prepare a 20 cm square baking tray by greasing and lining with non-stick baking paper.

1. Place Nuttelex and sweetened condensed soy milk in a small saucepan and stir constantly over low heat until mixture has melted and is smooth.
2. Remove from heat and add lemon juice. Combine well.
3. Finely crush biscuits by placing in a plastic snap-lock bag and rolling with rolling pin.

4. Combine crushed biscuits and coconut together in a large bowl.
5. Add melted mixture to dry ingredients and stir until well combined.
6. Press mixture into prepared pan using the back of a metal spoon or wet clean hands.
7. Prepare lemon icing (see p. 116) and spread over slice. Sprinkle with extra coconut.
8. Refrigerate until cold and firm then cut into pieces.

cherry ripe slice

A no-bake slice popular with children and great for parties.

Preparation time: 30 minutes
Servings: About 25 slices

....

½ cup copha
1 quantity sweetened condensed soy milk (see pages 113 and 114)
Pink food colouring
2½ cups (about 250 g) dairy-free, nut-free, egg-free (and gluten-free)
     plain sweet biscuits
½ cup glace cherries, chopped
1 cup desiccated coconut
1 cup (about 140 g) dairy-free, nut-free chocolate pieces

....

Grease and line a 20 cm square baking tray with non-stick baking paper.

1. In a small saucepan whisk copha and sweetened condensed soy milk over low
    heat until melted and combined.
2. Remove from heat and add food colouring. Stir well.
3. Finely crush biscuits by placing in a plastic snap-lock bag and rolling with
    rolling pin.

4. Combine crushed biscuits, cherries and coconut in a large bowl and mix together.
5. Stir melted mixture into dry ingredients and combine well.
6. Press mixture firmly into tray using back of metal spoon or wet clean hands.
7. Break the chocolate into small pieces and place in small heatproof bowl. Microwave on high for 1 minute. Stir well to combine. If not quite melted, heat for further intervals of 30 seconds on high until completely melted.
8. Spread chocolate over slice and refrigerate until set. Cut into slices.

crunchy ginger slice

This crunchy slice has a lovely chewy topping.

Preparation time: 30 minutes
Servings: About 20 pieces

....

½ cup Nuttelex (or other dairy-free spread), (plus 2 tablespoons extra)
⅓ cup sugar
1 cup SR flour (or gluten-free SR flour)
1 teaspoon ground ginger (plus 1 teaspoon extra)
3 teaspoons golden syrup
⅓ cup icing sugar

....

Preheat oven to 180°C and grease and line a 20 cm square baking tray with non-stick baking paper.

1. Mix Nuttelex and sugar together in a large bowl with a large metal spoon until well combined (use back of spoon to push mix together).
2. Add flour and ginger and mix well.
3. Press into prepared tray in a thin layer using back of metal spoon and bake for 15–20 minutes or until lightly browned.
4. In a small saucepan stir golden syrup, icing sugar, extra ginger and extra Nuttelex until melted and well combined.
5. Pour warm topping over warm biscuit base.
6. Cool slice in tray then cut into slices.

fruity slice

A delicious accompaniment to your morning cuppa.

Preparation time: 30 minutes
Servings: About 25 squares

1 quantity sweetened condensed soy milk (see pages 113 and 114)
2 cups dried mixed fruit
1 cup SR flour

Preheat oven to 160°C and grease and line a 20 cm square tray with non-stick baking paper.

1. Mix all ingredients in a large bowl.
2. Spread into prepared slice tray.
3. Bake for 35–40 minutes, or until a skewer inserted into slice comes out clean.
4. Allow to cool in tray then cut into squares.

chocolate
balls

Always a favourite and easy for the kids to make. They are best stored in an airtight container in the refrigerator, but also freeze well when stored in a sealed freezer-safe container. Remember to thaw at room temperature for about 30 minutes prior to serving.

Preparation time: 20 minutes
Servings: About 30 balls

....

2½ cups (about 250 g) dairy-free, nut-free, egg-free (and gluten-free)
    plain sweet biscuits
2 tablespoons cocoa
1 cup desiccated coconut (plus extra)
1 quantity sweetened condensed soy milk (see pages 113 and 114)

....

Prepare a biscuit tray by lining with non-stick baking paper.

1. Finely crush biscuits by placing in a plastic snap-lock bag and rolling with rolling pin.
2. In a large bowl mix crushed biscuits with all other ingredients.
3. Roll teaspoons of mixture into balls and then roll in extra coconut.
4. Place balls on prepared tray and place in refrigerator until cold and firm.

apricot balls

These are best stored in an airtight container in the refrigerator. They also freeze well when stored in a sealed freezer-safe container and are best when thawed at room temperature for at least 30 minutes prior to serving.

Preparation time: 30 minutes
Servings: About 36 balls

2 cups dried apricots, finely chopped
2½ cups desiccated coconut
I cup sweetened condensed soy milk (see pages 113 and 114)

Prepare a biscuit tray by lining with non-stick baking paper.

1. Combine all ingredients in a large bowl and mix together well.
2. Roll teaspoons of mixture into balls and then roll in extra coconut.
3. Place on prepared tray and refrigerate until cold and firm.

fast desserts

In this section . . .

very fast pancakes

These freeze well and are great for school lunchboxes or afternoon snacks. They are great with maple syrup, stewed fruit or any other topping you like! If making the gluten-free version, let the batter rest for 5 minutes to thicken slightly prior to use.

Preparation time: 5 minutes
Servings: About 8 medium or 10 pikelet size

dry
1 cup SR flour
2 tablespoons caster sugar

wet
1 cup soy milk
2 tablespoons vegetable oil
1 teaspoon vanilla essence

1. Combine all dry ingredients in a medium bowl and mix together.
2. Make a well in centre of dry ingredients and add wet ingredients. Whisk together until they form a smooth batter.
3. Preheat a pan to medium heat and lightly spray with cooking spray. Place spoonfuls of batter in pan. Small spoonfuls are good for pikelets, use larger spoonfuls for pancakes.
4. Flip the pancakes when you see bubbles in the middle or if the edges start to look firm. They should be golden brown underneath.
5. Brown on other side then serve with your favourite topping.

chocolate fudge pudding

Everyone will come back for seconds of this yummy dessert.

Preparation time: 20 minutes
Servings: About 4 servings

....

1 cup SR flour
2 tablespoons cocoa (plus ¼ cup extra)
¾ cup sugar
½ cup soy milk
1 teaspoon vanilla essence
1½ tablespoons Nuttelex (or other dairy-free spread), melted
¾ cup brown sugar
1¾ cups hot water

....

Preheat oven to 180°C and grease a deep ovenproof pudding dish (about 2 litre size).

1. Combine flour, cocoa and sugar in a large bowl and mix together.
2. Make a well in the centre of the dry ingredients and stir in soy milk, vanilla and melted Nuttelex until smooth.
3. Pour into prepared ovenproof dish.
4. Sift brown sugar and extra cocoa together evenly over top of the pudding mixture.
5. Pour hot water gently over top of pudding (pour over the back of a metal spoon).
6. Bake for 50 minutes or until a skewer inserted into cake section comes out clean.

fruit crumble

A delicious winter treat.

Preparation time: 20 minutes
Servings: 4 large serves

....

1 can (400 g) fruit (e.g. pie apples, peaches, apricots)
1 tablespoon caster sugar
1 teaspoon cinnamon
½ cup SR flour
2 tablespoons Nuttelex (or other dairy-free spread), straight from the fridge
2 tablespoons desiccated coconut
¼ cup brown sugar

....

Preheat oven to 180°C and grease an ovenproof pudding dish (about 2 litre size).

1. Place fruit in prepared dish.
2. Sprinkle with caster sugar and cinnamon.
3. Place flour into small bowl. Cut cold Nuttelex into small pieces and rub into flour mixture with fingertips until it resembles fine breadcrumbs and no large pieces of Nuttelex remain.
4. Add coconut and brown sugar to mix and combine well.
5. Sprinkle crumble mixture over apples.
6. Bake for 25–30 minutes or until topping starts to brown.

golden syrup dumplings

This traditional winter favourite can be made a day ahead and reheated in your microwave before eating.

Preparation time: 20 minutes
Servings: About 8 dumplings

3 cups water
I cup brown sugar
⅓ cup golden syrup
⅓ cup Nuttelex (or other dairy-free spread)
I cup SR flour
¼ cup Nuttelex (extra, straight from fridge)
I tablespoon golden syrup (extra)
½ cup soy milk

1. In a large wide saucepan combine water, sugar, golden syrup and Nuttelex. Stir constantly over low heat until melted and well combined.
2. Place flour in a medium bowl. Cut cold extra Nuttelex into small pieces and rub into flour mixture with fingertips until it resembles fine breadcrumbs and no large pieces of Nuttelex remain.
3. Add extra golden syrup and soy milk to flour mixture. Stir to combine well.
4. Increase heat on sauce so it starts to boil then use two dessertspoons to drop heaped spoonfuls of the mixture into the sauce in a single layer.
5. Cover and simmer for 10 minutes. Turn dumplings over and continue to cook for a further 5–10 minutes or until dumplings are firm to touch.

fruit charlotte

A great way to use up your stale bread.

Preparation time: 20 minutes
Servings: 4 large serves

....

10–12 slices stale bread (or gluten-free stale bread)
¼ cup Nuttelex (or other dairy-free spread)
1 can (400 g) fruit (e.g. pie apples, peaches, apricots)
1 tablespoon caster sugar
1 teaspoon cinnamon
Cinnamon sugar

....

Preheat oven to 190°C and grease a medium ovenproof pudding dish
(about 2 litre size).

1. Remove crusts from bread and cut to fit base, sides and top of dish, ensuring
   there are no gaps.
2. Spread bread with Nuttelex and place into the dish Nuttelex side down.
3. Spread fruit over bread.
4. Sprinkle caster sugar and cinnamon over fruit.
5. Enclose with remaining bread slices, Nuttelex side up.
6. Bake for 30 minutes or until light brown and crispy.
7. Sprinkle with cinnamon sugar to serve.

warm toffee apples

This dessert is delicious served with soy ice-cream.

Preparation time: 15 minutes
Servings: 4

....

2 medium firm apples (e.g. Granny Smith)
2 tablespoons Nuttelex (or other dairy-free spread)
2 tablespoons caster sugar
¼ cup maple syrup

....

1. Peel apples and remove the core.
2. Slice the apples across the centre into thin slices.
3. In a pan, melt the Nuttelex and place apple slices in a single layer.
4. Cook apple until browned then turn to brown other side.
5. Sprinkle caster sugar over apples in the pan and cook until the sugar is melted and toffee starts to form around apple.
6. Add the maple syrup to pan and stir until heated through.
7. Place apples in serving bowls and drizzle with toffee syrup.

mango fritters

Try replacing the mango with banana for a change. If making the gluten-free version, there is no need to refrigerate batter prior to use. These delicious fritters are best made just prior to serving.

Preparation time: 20 minutes
Servings: 4

....

2 large mangoes
1 cup plain flour (or gluten-free plain flour)
1 cup water
Vegetable oil
⅓ cup honey

....

1. Peel mangoes and cut into wedges.
2. Place flour and water in a medium bowl and whisk together until smooth.
3. Cover with cling wrap and refrigerate for 15 minutes until slightly thickened.
4. Half fill a large saucepan with oil and carefully heat. Check if the oil is ready by putting a drop of batter in the pan and waiting until it bubbles and rises to the top.
5. Remove batter from refrigerator and stir well.
6. Take each piece of mango and dip into batter. Allow excess to drain before placing small batches in hot oil for 2 minutes or until crispy and golden brown.
7. Drain cooked pieces on paper towels.
8. Warm honey by placing in a large mug in microwave on high for 20 seconds.
9. Place fritters into serving bowls and drizzle with warmed honey.

baked bananas

Preparation time: 10 minutes
Servings: 4

4 medium bananas
½ cup honey
2 tablespoons water
2 tablespoons lemon juice

Preheat oven to 200°C and grease a shallow 20 cm baking tray.

1. Peel and cut the bananas in half lengthwise and place in prepared tray.
2. In a small bowl combine honey, water and juice.
3. Pour over bananas.
4. Bake for 15 minutes, basting halfway through cooking.
5. Remove from oven and cool slightly before serving.

icy
bananas

These banana 'icy poles' are a great healthy treat to serve at children's parties. Make the day before and once frozen, store in an airtight container in the freezer.

Preparation time: 10 minutes
Servings: 4

....

4 small ripe bananas
¼ cup orange juice
I cup rice bubbles (or gluten-free rice bubbles)

....

Prepare a biscuit tray by lining with non-stick baking paper.

1. Place the rice bubbles into a snap-lock bag and lightly crush with a rolling pin. Place crushed bubbles onto a plate.
2. Pour orange juice into a shallow dish.
3. Peel bananas and dip in juice then roll in crushed bubbles.
4. Insert an icy pole stick or skewer into bottom of banana until secure.
5. Place on prepared tray and freeze for about 30 minutes until firm.

choc-dipped strawberries

These are best made on the day of serving.

Preparation time: 15 minutes
Servings: About 12 berries

. . . .

1 punnet strawberries
1½ cups (200 g) dairy-free, nut-free chocolate pieces
Sprinkles (or gluten-free sprinkles)

. . . .

Prepare a biscuit tray by lining with non-stick baking paper.

1. Wash and thoroughly dry strawberries.
2. Melt chocolate by placing small pieces in heatproof bowl in microwave for 1 minute on high. Stir well and, if needed, heat again in intervals of 30 seconds on high until completely melted.
3. Place sprinkles in a small bowl.
4. Half dip strawberries in melted chocolate then roll in sprinkles.
5. Place on prepared tray and refrigerate until set.

chocolate sprinkle mallows

An extremely quick treat that kids love to help make. These can be made the day before serving if required and stored in an airtight container in the refrigerator.

Preparation time: 15 minutes
Servings: About 20 marshmallows

....

1 packet of marshmallows (or gluten-free marshmallows)
Toothpicks
1½ cups (200 g) dairy-free, nut-free chocolate
Sprinkles (or gluten-free sprinkles)

....

Prepare a biscuit tray by lining with non-stick baking paper.

1. Place toothpicks in as many marshmallows as required.
2. Melt chocolate by placing small pieces in heatproof bowl in microwave for 1 minute on high. Stir well and, if needed, heat again in intervals of 30 seconds on high until completely melted.
3. Place sprinkles in a small bowl.
4. Dip marshmallows in melted chocolate then roll in sprinkles.
5. Place on prepared tray and refrigerate until set.

marshmallow fruit sticks

gluten free option

These popular additions to children's parties are best made close to time of serving. Use any fruit firm enough to stay on the skewer.

Preparation time: 20 minutes
Servings: 15 small skewers

....

1 packet of marshmallows (or gluten-free marshmallows)
Strawberries
Grapes
Small skewers (or cut large ones in half, ensuring no sharp ends)

....

Prepare a biscuit tray by lining with non-stick baking paper.

1. Thread one strawberry, one marshmallow and one grape onto skewers.
2. Place on prepared tray and store in refrigerator until ready to serve.

marshmallow snowballs

gluten free option

These party treats can be made the day before serving if required. They are best stored in an airtight container in the refrigerator.

Preparation time: 20 minutes
Servings: About 20 marshmallows

1 packet of marshmallows (or gluten-free marshmallows)
1½ cups (200 g) dairy-free, nut-free chocolate
Desiccated coconut

Prepare a biscuit tray by lining with non-stick baking paper.

1. Melt chocolate by placing small pieces in heatproof bowl in microwave for 1 minute on high. Stir well and, if needed, heat again in intervals of 30 seconds on high until completely melted.
2. Place coconut in a small bowl.
3. Dip marshmallows in melted chocolate then roll in coconut.
4. Place on prepared tray and refrigerate until set.

fairy bread

This is best made close to time of serving.

Preparation time: 15 minutes
Servings: As many as desired

Sliced white bread (or gluten-free sliced white bread)
Nuttelex (or other dairy-free spread)
Sprinkles (or gluten-free sprinkles)

1. Spread Nuttelex onto one side of bread.
2. Shake sprinkles on top.
3. Cut each slice into halves or quarters or alternatively use cookie cutters to cut shapes out of the bread.

sprinkle buttons

These homemade chocolate freckles are best stored in an airtight container in the refrigerator.

Preparation time: 15 minutes
Servings: About 40 small buttons

¾ cup (about 100 g) dairy-free, nut-free chocolate pieces
Sprinkles (or gluten-free sprinkles)

1. Line a baking tray with greaseproof paper.
2. Melt chocolate by breaking into small pieces and placing in heatproof bowl in microwave for 1 minute on high. Stir well and, if needed, heat again in intervals of 30 seconds on high until completely melted.
3. Using a teaspoon, place small mounds of melted chocolate onto lined tray.
4. Stop spooning every 30 seconds or so to shake sprinkles on top before the chocolate sets.
5. Once all chocolate has been used, place in refrigerator to set.

little extras

In this section . . .

rich chocolate sauce

This is a lovely rich, thick sauce that is great over soy ice-cream and can be served warm or cold. It can be stored in the refrigerator for a few days and mixed with cold soy milk to make a thinner consistency if desired.

Preparation time: 10 minutes
Servings: About 1½ cups

. . . .

¼ cup sugar
⅓ cup cocoa
3 tablespoons cornflour (or gluten-free cornflour)
½ cup water
½ cup soy milk

. . . .

1. Combine all ingredients in a small saucepan and whisk until smooth.
2. Whisk over low heat until thickened but do not boil.

caramel sauce

This is a deliciously sweet thin sauce that keeps well in the refrigerator for a few days.

Preparation time: 15 minutes
Servings: About ¾ cup

¼ cup Nuttelex (or other dairy-free spread)
1 tablespoon golden syrup
¼ cup brown sugar
2 tablespoons sweetened condensed soy milk (see pages 113 and 114)
¼ cup water

1. In a medium saucepan combine Nuttelex, golden syrup, sugar, sweetened condensed soy milk and water.
2. Whisk over low heat until melted.
3. Continue to whisk while simmering for a few minutes then remove from heat.

sweetened condensed soy milk using soy milk

gluten free option

This easy alternative, which can be made in advance and stored in the refrigerator, replaces sweetened condensed milk in a variety of recipes. If taken from the refrigerator, mix well prior to use or it will become firm.

Preparation time: 15 minutes
Servings: Equivalent to one 400 g can

....

3 tablespoons cornflour (or gluten-free cornflour)
2 tablespoons cold water
¾ cup soy milk
½ cup white sugar
3 tablespoons Nuttelex (or other dairy-free spread)

....

1. Place cornflour in a cup and blend with cold water to make a thin watery paste. Always add water to cornflour, not the other way around or it turns lumpy.
2. In a small saucepan place soy milk, sugar, Nuttelex and cornflour mixture.
3. Use a whisk to stir constantly over low to medium heat until the mixture thickens. As soon as it thickens, remove from heat.
4. Cool before using (can place in fridge or freezer to speed up the cooling if required).

sweetened condensed soy milk using soy milk powder

gluten free option

This is a simple method of making condensed soy milk and has the bonus of not needing a saucepan. As with the previous recipe, this can be made in advance and stored in the refrigerator for use in a variety of recipes. If taken from the refrigerator, mix well prior to use or it will become firm.

Preparation time: 15 minutes
Servings: Equivalent to one 400 g can

....

1 cup dry soy milk powder
⅔ cup white sugar
3 tablespoons Nuttelex (or other dairy-free spread)
½ cup boiling water

....

1. Place soy milk powder, sugar and Nuttelex in a large bowl.
2. Whisk boiling water into all other ingredients until smooth.

simple sugar icing

Preparation time: 5 minutes

....

1 ½ cups icing sugar (or gluten-free icing sugar)
1–1 ½ tablespoons boiling water
Food colouring

....

1. Place icing sugar in a bowl.
2. Add water to icing and mix well until smooth.
3. Add desired food colouring.
4. If icing is too watery, add more icing sugar. If icing is too firm, add more water.

lemon or orange icing

Preparation time: 5 minutes

....

1½ cups icing sugar (or gluten-free icing sugar)
2 tablespoons lemon juice or orange juice

....

1. Place icing sugar into a medium bowl.
2. Add juice and stir until smooth and well combined.
3. If icing is too watery, add more icing sugar. If icing is too firm, add more juice.

chocolate icing

Preparation time: 5 minutes

....

1½ cups icing sugar (or gluten-free icing sugar)
2 tablespoons cocoa
2–2½ tablespoons boiling water

....

1. Place icing sugar and cocoa into a medium bowl and mix.
2. Add water and stir until smooth and well combined.
3. If icing is too watery, add more icing sugar. If icing is too firm, add more water.

butter-
cream icing

gluten free option

Once cake or biscuits have been iced, store in the refrigerator to keep icing firm.

Preparation time: 10 minutes

....

1½ cups icing sugar (or gluten-free icing sugar)
1–1½ tablespoons soy milk
⅓ cup Nuttelex (or other dairy-free spread)
Food colouring
Food flavouring

....

1. Place icing sugar in a large bowl.
2. Make well in centre and add soy milk and softened Nuttelex.
3. Mix slowly by using back of metal spoon to press sugar into spread. Combine well until smooth.
4. If icing is too watery, add more icing sugar. If icing is too firm, add more soy milk.
5. Add any desired colouring or flavouring.

chocolate-cream icing

gluten free option

This icing is delicious. Once biscuits or cake have been iced, store in the refrigerator to keep icing firm.

Preparation time: 10 minutes

1½ cups icing sugar (or gluten-free icing sugar)
¼ cup cocoa
2 tablespoons soy milk
⅓ cup Nuttelex (or other dairy-free spread)

1. Place icing sugar and cocoa into a large bowl and mix well.
2. Make well in centre and add soy milk and softened Nuttelex.
3. Mix slowly by using back of metal spoon to press sugar into spread. Combine well until smooth.
4. If icing is too watery, add more icing sugar. If icing is too firm, add more soy milk.

orange-
cream icing

Preparation time: 10 minutes

....

2 cups icing sugar (or gluten-free icing sugar)
½ cup Nuttelex (or other dairy-free spread)
2 tablespoons orange juice
1 teaspoon orange rind, finely grated

....

1. Place icing sugar in a large bowl.
2. Make well in centre and add softened Nuttelex and juice.
3. Mix slowly by using back of metal spoon to press sugar into spread.
   Combine well until smooth.
4. Stir orange rind through icing.
5. If icing is too watery, add more icing sugar. If icing is too firm, add more juice.

honey
icing

Preparation time: 10 minutes

....

1½ cups icing sugar (or gluten-free icing sugar)
1 tablespoon Nuttelex (or other dairy-free spread)
1 tablespoon honey
2–3 teaspoons boiling water

....

1. Place icing sugar into a medium bowl.
2. Melt Nuttelex and honey together in small heatproof bowl by placing in microwave on high for 20 seconds.
3. Add melted mixture and boiling water to icing sugar.
4. Stir until smooth and combined well.
5. If icing is too watery, add more icing sugar. If icing is too firm, add more hot water.

index

Wakefield Press is an independent publishing and
distribution company based in Adelaide, South Australia.
We love good stories and publish beautiful books.
To see our full range of titles, please visit our website at
www.wakefieldpress.com.au.